The Syriac Orthodox Celebration of the Eucharist in Light of Jacob of Serugh's *Mimro* 95

Analecta Gorgiana

1046

Series Editor

George Anton Kiraz

Analecta Gorgiana is a collection of long essays and short monographs which are consistently cited by modern scholars but previously difficult to find because of their original appearance in obscure publications. Carefully selected by a team of scholars based on their relevance to modern scholarship, these essays can now be fully utilized by scholars and proudly owned by libraries.

The Syriac Orthodox Celebration of the Eucharist in Light of Jacob of Serugh's *Mimro* 95

Amir Harrak

gorgias press
2011

Gorgias Press LLC, 954 River Road, Piscataway, NJ, 08854, USA

www.gorgiaspress.com

Copyright © 2011 by Gorgias Press LLC

Originally published in 2010

All rights reserved under International and Pan-American Copyright Conventions. No part of this publication may be reproduced, stored in a retrieval system or transmitted in any form or by any means, electronic, mechanical, photocopying, recording, scanning or otherwise without the prior written permission of Gorgias Press LLC.

2011 ܟܒ

ISBN 978-1-4632-0094-7   ISSN 1935-6854

Reprinted from the 2010 Piscataway edition.

Printed in the United States of America

THE SYRIAC ORTHODOX CELEBRATION OF THE EUCHARIST IN LIGHT OF JACOB OF SERUGH'S *MIMRŌ* 95

AMIR HARRAK

I. INTRODUCTION

In his magnificent poetical way, the poet theologian Jacob of Serugh (452–521) discussed the Eucharist, not simply as a theological subject but as a ritual of prime importance in the Christian life. In his hymn entitled *On the Partaking of the Holy Mysteries*, *mimrō* 95 of his large metrical repertoire,[1] Jacob exhorts, entices, and teaches his readers to attend the Eucharist celebration, not to leave it because it is too long, but to benefit from its spiritual nourishments. In doing so, Jacob provides us with unique information on how the Eucharist was celebrated during his own time, which was slightly different from the current celebration of the same within the Syriac Orthodox Church. Before discussing his references to the Eucharistic celebration, let us survey expressions that highlight his concept of the Eucharist, so as to better understand why he devoted a whole *mimrō* to the topic.

---

[1] Bedjan, Paulus, ed. *Homiliae Selectae Mar-Jacobi Serughensis*, vol. III, 646–63, Leipzig: William Drugulin, 1902; repr. Gorgias Press, 2006. See also *Metrical Homilies of Mar Jacob of Serugh: Jacob of Serugh's Homily on the Partaking of the Holy Mysteries*, trans. and introd. by Amir Harrak, Texts from Christian Late Antiquity, 23.17, Gorgias Press, 2009.

II. NAMES OF THE EUCHARIST IN JACOB OF SERUGH

Jacob calls the Eucharist by several names, all familiar in Syriac literature. The main name is *pōṯūrō* "Table:"

Come and be fattened by the Table full of life,
for its food cannot be spoiled for the one who deserves it (2).[2]

The Table is often that "of the Church" (24), or a "Spiritual Table" (3)," Divine Table," (160), and "Table of the Royal Groom" (6). The Eucharist is also *ḥlūlō* "wedding banquet":

The bride of the King made a wedding feast for the children of her Mysteries
and with them she begs that she may rejoice today tremendously (5).

He has set at the wedding feast his body and blood before the reclining ones
that they may eat of him and live with him without end (181).

Terms related to banqueting include *smōḵō*, *ḥšomīṯō*, and *šōrūṯō*, as subsequently illustrated:

Come, my dear ones, and recline in a spiritual *smōḵō*-feast,
for love calls you concerning its divine actions (3).

---

[2] Digits between brackets refer to stanzas (not to lines) in *mimrō* 95.

At the heads of streets and in the corners of the earth (the Bride of the King) stood up,
calling toward her assemblies and crowds for the *ḥšomīṯō*-banquet (8).

ܠܡܢ ܫܥ̈ܝܐ ܕܥܕܬܐ ܚܫܝܒܝܢ ܠܗ ܒܛܠܢܐ܀
ܠܡܢ ܬܫܡܫܬܐ ܠܐ ܚܫܝܒܐ ܠܗ ܐܝܟ ܫܘܪܘܬܐ܀

Why are the Hours of the church considered idleness?
Why is not the liturgical service considered a *šōrūṯō*-meal? (59)

ܠܐ ܬܬܪܗܒܘܢ ܠܡܫܬܢܝܘ ܡܢ ܫܘܪܘܬܐ܀
ܕܥܒܕܬ ܟܠܬܐ ܠܥܠܡܐ ܟܠܗ ܢܬܒܣܡ ܒܗ܀

Do not rush to take your leave from the *šōrūṯō*-meal,
which the Bride has made so that the entire world may take delight in it (93).

Sacrificial offering, *qurbōnō*, and oblation, *debeḥṯō*, are also attested:

ܐܡܪܘ ܠܗ ܠܐܒܐ ܗܐ ܒܪܟ ܕܒܚܬܐ ܕܪܥܝܐ ܠܟ܀
ܒܗܘ ܫܒܘܩ ܕܢܫܬܒܩ ܚܠܦܝ ܐܬܢܟܣ ܒܗ܀

Say to the Father: Behold, your Son is an oblation that pleases you!
Forgive me through him, for he died on my behalf that I may be forgiven through him (162).

ܗܐ ܩܘܪܒܢܟ ܩܒܠ ܡܢ ܐܝܕܝ ܕܐܝܬܘܗܝ ܡܢܟ
ܘܐܬܪܥܐ ܒܗ ܕܗܢܘ ܐܝܬ ܠܝ ܕܐܩܪܒ ܠܟ܀

Behold your sacrifice: Accept it from my hands for He comes from you!
Be pleased by Him for this is what I have to offer you (163).

The familiar but charged term *rōzē* "mysteries" is also present:

ܡܐ ܕܡܫܬܡܫܝܢ ܗܠܝܢ ܐ̈ܪܙܐ ܕܡܠܝܢ ܚ̈ܝܐ܀
ܗܘܝܘ ܡܥܒܕ ܥܠ ܥ̈ܠܠܬܐ ܕܟܠ ܚܘܣܪ̈ܢܐ܀

When these *rōzē*-mysteries, full of life, are administered,
He (=Satan) fabricates motives leading to all sorts of losses (121).

ܘܡܛܠ ܗܢܐ ܚܫܝܫ ܣܛܢܐ ܘܡܨܛܠܐ ܚܫܝܫ܀
ܢܦܩ ܐܢܫܐ ܡܢ ܒܝܬ ܡܘܕܥܐ ܒܥܕܢ ܐ̈ܪܙܐ܀

On this account, Satan is concerned and is much anxious
to drive people out of the church during the time of the *rōzē*-mysteries (127).

Finally, the more general but usual term *tešmeštō* "service" is as popular as *pōṭūrō* "table" encountered above:

> When you pass by, do not, as usual, turn aside when you draw near to us,
> So that the call of the Service is ineffectual in bringing you here (36).

> Plant your lives in the Service full of mysteries,
> So that you may bear sweet fruits of glory for the Lord of Eden (76).

> Life springs from the Service of the house of God.
> O lovers of life, abstain not from its benefits (77).

> Why are the Hours of the church considered idleness?
> Why is not the liturgical service considered a *šōrūṭō*-meal? (59)

III. STAGES OF THE LITURGY IN LIGHT OF JACOB'S *MIMRŌ* 95

Part of *mimrō* 95 reflects the various stages of the Syriac Orthodox liturgy of his time while the other parts comment, almost in a mystical way, on the value and worthiness of the Eucharist to the Christian. The *mimrō* can be divided as follows:

1–4: Call to the theme
5–9: The Church is a banquet
10–23: The Body of Christ is a source
24–26: The Church is the place of peace
27–56: Exhortations to attend the Church, the liturgy is a healing
57–64: Call to the repentant
65–95: *Stages of the Liturgy*
96–101: Concept of baptism
102–182: *Stages of the Liturgy*

Jacob refers to the various sections of the Eucharist celebration as part of his general discussion of the Partaking of the Holy Mysteries and does not treat them independently. That he refers to them successively is, however, clear from the fact that his relevant discussion corresponds in large part to the current celebration of the Eucharistic liturgy in the Syriac Orthodox Church. The Syriac Orthodox liturgy can be divided into two major parts: The Pre-Anaphoric Service, also called the Service of the Word, and the Anaphora proper, that is the Eucharistic Service proper.

III.1. The Pre-Anaphoric Service

The offerings are prepared and the incense is served in this service, attended by both the catechumens and the faithful. It is a preparatory service as its Syriac name, ܛܟܣܐ ܕܩܘܪܒܐ ܕܛܘܝܒܐ "Preparatory Service of the Eucharist," suggests. Among the rituals performed in this service is the burning of the incense and the readings from the Holy Scriptures—subsequently Psalms and Prophets from the Old Testament, Acts, Catholic Epistles, Epistles of St. Paul, and the Gospels from the New Testament. This service used to take place on the *bīmō*, a platform in the middle of the church, though this architectural structure disappeared probably after the 14th century.[3] All these constituents of the *Liturgy of the Word*, in addition to *madrōšē* sang by virgins, are referred to by Jacob as follows:

---

[3] The latest *bīmō* is attested in a Syriac Orthodox monastic church uncovered in the vicinity of Takrit. The latest date attested there is the first quarter of the 13th century; see Harrak, A. "Recent Archaeological Excavations in Takrit and the Discovery of Syriac Inscriptions," *Journal of the CSSS* 1 (2001): 14, and plans 1, 2, and 3. An extremely well preserved *bīmō*, built with stones and mortar, has been recently unearthed by Iraqi archaeologists in Bazyan, near Sulaimaniyya, in Iraqi Kurdistan; see Ali, Narmen Muhammad Amen. "The 'Monastic Church' of Bāzyān, in Iraqi Kurdistan," *Journal of the CSSS* 8 (2008): 74–84.

Scriptures and *madrōšē*:

Be patient and listen to the tunes of the Psalms
that the prophetic finger struck on the words of David (65).

Pay heed to the *madrōšē*-hymns (sung) by the virgins with glorious voices
that the wisdom of the Most High has given to the congregations (66).

Listen to the Prophets, who like pipes of pure gold
Pour forth life from their mouths into the ears of man (67).

Pay heed to the Apostles, who like running rivers
force their way to water the royal Paradise with magnificent streams (68).

Bema

Turn your ear toward the divine *bīmō*,
And receive from it precious pearls (69).

Beneficial Scriptures

Learn and believe that the Testaments are rivers.
For in both of them you have life that has no end (70).

Listen to the New and pay heed to the Old, and realize
that in both one and same truth is spoken to you (71).

Behold, you hear from the Old Testament that four rivers
run from the blessed source of Eden (72),

ܘܬܘܒ ܒܚܕܬܐ ܫܠܝ̈ܚܐ ܒܕܡܘܬ ܢܗܪ̈ܘܬܐ.
ܐܪܒܥܐ ܕܢܦܩܘ ܠܐܪܒܥ ܦܢܝ̈ܢ ܐܪܘܘ ܐܢܝܢ܀

and then in the New Testament (that) the Apostles like four rivers
went out to the four corners (of the world), watering them (73):

ܥܕܝܢ ܓܓܘܠܬܐ ܗܝ، ܘܡܣܒܪ̈ܢܐ ܢܗܪ̈ܘܬܐ:
ܐܪܒܥܐ ܢܦܩܘ ܗܘܘ ܠܐܪܒܥ ܦܢܝܢ ܘܐܪܘܝܘ ܐܢܝܢ܀

Eden is Golgotha, and the Evangelists are the rivers,
the four went out to the four corners and made them rejoice (Ms B).

Dismissal of the Catechumens:

ܠܐ ܬܦܘܩ ܠܟ ܡܐ ܕܡܬܩܕܫ ܒܝܬ ܩܘܕܫܐ:
ܕܒܪ ܒܝܬܐ ܐܢ̄ܬ ܠܘ ܢܘܟܪܝܐ ܕܬܫܢܐ ܠܟ܀

Do not depart when the Sanctification begins in the Holy of Holies,
for you are of the Household and not a stranger (who must) move out! (94)

ܡܐ ܕܫܡܥܬ ܐܢ̄ܬ ܕܐܝܢܐ ܕܠܐ ܩܒܠ ܪܘܫܡܐ ܢܐܙܠ.
ܐܢ̄ܬ ܠܐ ܬܐܙܠ ܕܪܫܝܡܐ ܐܢ̄ܬ ܐܦ ܒܪܒܝܬܐ܀

When you hear: "Let the one who did not receive the signing (*rušmō*) leave,"
you ought not to leave since you are signed and are a family member (95).

ܒܪܘܫܡܐ ܪܫܝܡܬ ܒܟܠܝܠܐ ܟܠܝܠܬ ܒܐܚ̈ܐ ܟܬܝܒ ܐܢ̄ܬ.
ܠܡܢ ܢܦܩ ܐܢ̄ܬ ܥܡ ܠܐ ܪ̈ܫܝܡܐ ܐܝܟ ܚܣܝܪܐ܀

You are signed with the sign, you are marked with the mark, among the brothers you are written.
Why do you leave with the unsigned, like a deficient one? (97)

Dismissal of the catechumens and hearers:

ܒܡܫܚܐ ܪܫܡܘܟ ܘܒܨܠܝܒ ܢܘܗܪܐ ܪܫܝܡ ܦܪ̈ܨܘܦܟ.
ܘܠܐܝܢܐ ܕܠܐ ܪܫܝܡ ܐܝܟ ܕܪܫܝܡ ܐܢ̄ܬ ܐܡܪܝܢ ܢܐܙܠ܀

They signed you with the oil, and your face is signed by the sign of the Cross of light,

but the one who is not signed the way you are signed, they ask
   to leave (100).

The sign of life made you a brother to the Only-Begotten One
and a son of his Father, and since you are in the household, do
   not leave! (101)

Remain inside the gate and call the Father: Our Father!
Because you are a son, you are permitted to call: Our father! (102)

On account of this, they put out he who is not baptized once
   the Sanctification takes place,
for he is not permitted to call the heavenly One "Our father"
   (103).

He who is not baptized, his lot is not among the sons,
And if he calls the Father "Our Father" this would be a lie (104).

On account of this they say: "Let the one who did not receive
   the signing (*rušmō*) leave,"
That a lie may not be spoken among the true ones (105).

He who leaves with the Listeners (*šōmuʿē*), what would he do
when they search for him in the House and he is not there to
   call "Our Father"? (117)

III.2. Anaphoric Service

Sanctus

(Satan), in every way, by his craftiness, brings you outside (the church),
so that you may be removed from the crowds that chants: *Qaddīš*-Sanctus! (122)

Epiclesis

Along with the priest, the entire congregation petitions the Father
to send his Son to come down and settle on the oblation (*qurbōnō*) (113).

The Holy Spirit makes his power descend on the bread and wine,
sanctifying them and turning them into the Body and Blood (114).

And through his hovering (*rūḥōfō*) he mixes (*ḥōleṭ*) them in a holy way,
and sacramentally (*rōzōnō'iṯ*), they become one with him, as is writte [4] (116).

The one (who leaves) deprives himself of the hovering—no one else deprives him of it.
What does he gain in the market in which he errs? (118)

Catholic Prayer

---

[4] John 17: 11, 21.

On this account, Satan is concerned and is much anxious
to drive people out of the church during the time of Mysteries
(*rōzē*), (127)

lest, when the entire congregation cries out: Forgive my faults
(*šḇuq lī ḥawbay*),
the sinner also shows up to be acquitted (128).

Blessing and Peace

When the congregation begs for mercy from God,
even the sinners that are in it enrich themselves with His grace (131).

When the congregation begs the Father for mercy,
he does not withhold it, not even from the bad ones found therein (132).

Fraction and Signation

You may say: I will go and work until the time of the sanctification,
and when the gates are opened, I will go in and take (communion) (138).

O intelligent one, chase away these considerations and get rid of them;
let your soul take care of its wounds to treat them (139).

Behold: this is the time when the gate of the Great Physician is opened;

he treats freely, so bring in your sore that he may take care of it (143).

Pater Noster

The Holy Spirit makes his power descend on the bread and wine,
sanctifying them and turning them into the Body and Blood (114).

And everyone who is in the House, moved, will call: "Our Father!"
And the new sons sanctify him and bless him (115).

Final Exhortation by Jacob of Serugh (162–170)

Say to the Father, behold, your son is an oblation that pleases you!
Forgive me through him, for he died on my behalf so that I may be forgiven through him.

Behold your sacrifice: Accept it from my hands for He comes from you.
Be pleased by Him for this is what I have to offer you!

Behold: His pure blood is poured on Golgotha for my sake,
pleading for me, so accept my supplication for his sake.

Many are my sins but greater is your mercy! If you weigh them,
your mercy will prevail even over the mountains that you balance!

Consider the sins and consider the sacrifice on account of them;
The slaughtered sacrifice is much greater than the sins!

Because I sinned, your beloved one sustained the nails and the lance;
His suffering is able to please you so that I may live.

Though I have been redeemed, the Evil one has encircled me, shooting me with his arrows;
O King and my Saviour, encircle me too and heal my wounds.

My enemy is pressing and has killed me with the spear-head of iniquity;
pass judgment on the insolent one for me, for he is not finished with me.

The soul is small and its injury is not very great,
the compassion that heals the stricken ones is greater than it.

IV. COMMENTS

Mimrō 95 preserves several stages found in the traditional celebration of the Eucharist within the Syriac Orthodox Church (marked with X below), but not all of the stages are referred to, as the following chart indicates:[5]

---

[5] The division of the Syriac Orthodox liturgy of the Eucharist is based on the following references: Khouri-Sarkis, G. "Le 'propre' de la messe syrienne," *L'Orient Syrien* 1/4 (1956): 445–60, esp. 449–60;

Traditional Eucharistic Liturgy	***mimrō* 95**
PREPARATORY SERVICE ܛܟܣܐ ܕܩܘܪܒܐ ܕܡܛܟܣܢܘܬܐ	
Introduction = ܡܥܠܬܐ	
Vestment of Priest = Service of Aaron	
Offertory (before catechumens' service)	
PRE-ANAPHORIC SERVICE (on the bema)	
Psalms	X
Hymns ܡܕܪ̈ܫܐ	X
Liturgy of the Catechumens	
Old Testament = ܐܘܪܝܬܐ	X
Book of Acts	
Catholic Epistles	X
Epistle = ܫܠܝܚܐ	X
Gospel = ܐܘܢܓܠܝܘܢ	X
Dismissal of the Catechumens ܐܝܢܐ ܕܠܐ ܫܩܠ ܪܘܫܡܐ ܢܐܙܠ	X
ANAPHORIC SERVICE	
Introit Prayer = ܣܕܪܐ ܕܡܥܠܬܐ	
Creed	
Prayer of Peace	
Imposition of hands	
Sanctus ܩܕܝܫ	X
Anamnesis	
Epiclesis ܪܘܚܦܐ	X
Great Intercessions ܕܝܦܬ̈ܟܐ، ܩܘܪ̈ܝܐ	
Catholic Prayer ܨܠܘܬܐ ܕܬܘܠܝܬܗܘܢ	X
Blessing and Peace ܡܫܡܫܢܘܬ ܒܘܪܟܬܐ ܘܫܠܡܐ	X
Fraction and Signation ܩܨܝܐ ܘܪܘܫܡܐ	X
Pater Noster ܨܠܘܬܐ ܡܪܢܝܬܐ	X
Prayer ܐܒܐ ܕܩܘܫܬܐ	X

Traditional Eucharistic Liturgy	*mimrō* 95
Procession of the Eucharist ܐܘܗܐ ܕܐܪܙܐ ܩܕܝܫܐ	
Communion	
Dismissal = ܚܘܬܡܐ	

As can be seen, *mimrō* 95 covers most of the liturgy of the Eucharist despite the fact that its author never intended to turn his discourse into a commentary on the same.[6]

Pre-Anaphoric Service

This service, also called the Liturgy of the Word or the Liturgy of the Catechumens, was performed on the bema referred to by Jacob of Serugh in stanza 69. Jacob invites the readers to listen to the Psalms, which "the prophetic finger struck on the words of David." Psalms were part of the pre-anaphoric service up to the beginning of the anaphora. The Anaphora of the Twelve Apostles, dated probably before the christological controversies of the fourth century and still used in the Maronite, Assyrian, and Chaldean Churches, contains several psalms or portions of psalms. These were assigned to Sundays and feasts and were sung alternatively by those in and those out of the sanctuary.[7] Ps 24:9–10 (Lift up your heads, O gates…) was also chanted when the priest and the deacons moved from the bema toward the altar at which point the gates of the Sanctuary were opened. Although this ancient liturgical move is no longer included in the Syriac Orthodox ritual, it is part of the Armenian canons of the mass to this day.[8]

---

[6] For such a commentary in Syriac see Labourt, Hieronymus, ed. *Dionysius bar Ṣalībī: Exposito Liturgiae*, CSCO SS textus, series secunda, 93, Parisiis: E. Typographeo Reipublicae, 1903.

[7] *The Liturgy of the Holy Apostles Adai and Mari*, 1 note 3, Urmi: Press of the Archbishop of Canterbury Mission, 1890; repr. Gorgias Press 2002. For a detailed study of the anaphora, and its edition and translation, see Gelston, A. *The Eucharistic Prayer of Addai and Mari*, Oxford: Clarendon, 1992.

[8] Harrak, A. "The Liturgical Dimension of Syriac Epigraphy," *The Harp* 32 (2008): 16–20.

The *madrōšē*-hymns, "(sung) by the virgins with glorious voices," are also part of the ancient celebration of the Eucharist. According to stanza 66, many congregations had choirs made of such virgins. It is interesting to see the role of female singers so expressly highlighted by Jacob. He himself commented on Ephrem's insistence in using virgins in his choir: "The blessed Ephrem saw that the women were silent from praise and in his wisdom he decided it was right that they should sing out!"[9] Perhaps these hymns were chanted while the celebrants moved in procession toward the altar during the introit.[10]

The Service is also made of readings from the Bible: The Old Testament, more precisely the "Prophets" according to Jacob, Catholic Letters (*gawōnōyōthō*), including the Acts of the Apostles (*praksīs*), Letters of Paul (*šlīḥō*), and finally the Gospels (*ewangēlyūn*). The liturgy includes verses from psalms or prayers sung by the choir immediately before each of these readings are done, called *qḏōm ʿattīqō* "before the Old [Testament]), *qḏōm qeryōnō da-praksīs waḏ-Pawlōs* "Before the Acts and Paul," and *qḏōm ewangēlyūn* "before the Gospel". All these readings are referred to by Jacob, who confirms that they were done on the bema: "Turn your ear to the divine *bīmō*, receiving from it precious jewels."[11] From the *ʿattīqō*, three readings were done, which were not *lectio continua*,[12] as is indeed the case even in the contemporary liturgy. If today these readings are not made on Sundays, they still are part and parcel of the Eucharistic service in major feasts.

---

[9] For the translation and more on the choirs of virgins mentioned by Jacob of Serugh with regards to Ephrem the Syrian, see Brock, Sebastian. *St. Ephrem the Syrian: Hymns on Paradise*, 22–4, Crestwood, NY: St Vladimir's Seminary Press, 1990.

[10] Khouri-Sarkis, "Le 'propre' de la messe syrienne," 449. The author mentions that during this part of service, psalms were chanted in the Latin liturgy.

[11] On such payers see *The Bread Of Life: The Book of the Divine Liturgy According to the Rite of the Syrian Orthodox Church of Antioch*, 58, Ṭūr Leḇnōn, 2002.

[12] Khouri-Sarkis, "Le 'propre' de la messe syrienne," 452.

The Liturgy of the Word was attended by the faithful and the catechumens alike and was followed by the homily to which there is no reference in *mimrō* 95. In the early centuries of Syriac Christianity, the catechumens[13] used to be dismissed from the church after the homily, a practice that had disappeared from the Syriac Orthodox liturgy already in the time of Jacob of Edessa (died in 708).[14] The liturgy of the Church of the East (Assyrian and Chaldean) preserves the words of the dismissal but does not perform it either. In fact the dismissal of the catechumens was a normal practice in Christianity in the earliest centuries,[15] and it is a major theme in *mimrō* 95 (stanzas 95 and 105). Let us compare the wording in these stanzas 95 and 105 to that which is still used in the Church of the East:

ܐܝܢܐ ܕܠܐ ܫܩܝܠ ܪܘܫܡܐ ܢܐܙܠ

ܡܢ ܕܠܐ ܫܩܝܠܐ ܠܗ ܡܥܡܘܕܝܬܐ ܢܐܙܠ. ܡܢ ܕܠܐ ܢܣܒ ܠܗ ܪܘܫܡܐ ܕܚܝ̈ܐ ܢܐܙܠ.[16]

Does ܪܘܫܡܐ, lit. "signing," refer to the non baptized in general or to inadmissible Christians, such as publically known sinners? The term in the Church of the East seems to refer to two categories of people: the non-baptized, including the catechumen referred to in the expression ܕܠܐ ܫܩܝܠܐ ܠܗ ܡܥܡܘܕܝܬܐ "he who did not receive baptism," and an individual "who did not receive the signing of life" ܕܠܐ ܢܣܒ ܠܗ ܪܘܫܡܐ ܕܚܝ̈ܐ, an expression similar to Jacob's ܕܠܐ ܫܩܝܠ ܪܘܫܡܐ. Sarhad Jammo (now Chaldean Bishop) has studied the East Syriac wording and convincingly argued that

---

[13] These were called ܡܬܬܪܬܢ̈ܐ but this term is not used by Jacob; on this term and its meaning see *Dionysius bar Ṣalībī: Exposito Liturgiae*, 21, lines 21–5.

[14] See his Letter in ibid., 6, lines 14–22.

[15] On the practice in Eastern Churches see Madey, John, et al. *The Eucharistic Liturgy in the Christian East*, 210 (Assyrian and Chaldean Churches), 308 (Melkite Church), 335 (Armenian Church), Kottayam, Kerala, India: Prakasam Publications, 1982.

[16] For the wording see for example *Ṭaksā d-kahnē d-ʿedtā d-madhenḥā [Office of the Priests of the Church of the East]*, 13, Mosul, 1928; Chicago repr., 2002.

ܪܘܫܡܐ is the signing of the Christian penitent and not another expression denoting the non-baptized (if the latter were referred to, there would be redundancy in the dismissal formula). For Narsai (died in 502) and Timothy II (died in 1332) the "signing of life" meant a signing administered to heretics and schismatics in the liturgy of reconciliation with the Church.[17]

Unlike the early East Syriac authors, Jacob of Serugh clearly means by ܪܘܫܡܐ "baptism," and hence the expression ܕܠܐ ܩܒܠ ܪܘܫܡܐ signifies "the non-baptized one, the catechumen." The signing and baptism equation is clear in the following stanza 99:

ܪܘܫܡܗ ܕܡܠܟܐ ܡܥܡܘܕܝܬܐ ܗܝ، ܒܪ̄ܬ ܢܘܗܪܐ
ܘܠܒܫܬ ܗܘ̄ ܪܘܫܡܐ ܪܒܐ ܠܡܢ ܢܦܩ ܐܢ̄ܬ

Baptism, the daughter of light, is the sign of the King
Since you bear this great sign, why do you leave (the church)?

Moreover, the expression ܪܘܫܡܐ ܕܚ̈ܝܐ "signing of life" also refers to baptism as in stanzas 100 and 101:

ܒܡܫܚܐ ܪܫܡܘܟ ܘܒܨܠܝܒ ܢܘܗܪܐ ܪܫܝܡ ܦܪ̈ܨܘܦܟ:
ܘܠܐܝܢܐ ܕܠܐ ܪܫܝܡ ܐܝܟ ܕܪܫܝܡ ܐܢ̄ܬ ܐܡܪܝܢ ܢܐܙܠ܀
ܪܘܫܡܐ ܕܚ̈ܝܐ ܥܒܕܟ ܐܚܐ ܠܝܚܝܕܝܐ:
ܘܒܪܐ ܠܐܒܘܗܝ، ܘܒܒܝܬܐ ܐܝܬ ܠܐ ܬܦܘܩ ܠܟ܀

They signed you with the oil and your face is signed with the sign of the cross of light,
but the one who is not signed the way you are signed, they ask to leave (100).
The sign of life made you a brother of the Only-Begotten-One, and a son of his Father; and since you are in the household, do not leave! (101)

Jacob's concept of baptism as ܪܘܫܡܐ and ܪܘܫܡܐ ܕܚ̈ܝܐ is also found in the *Acts of Thomas* #150[18] and in Aphrahat's

[17] Hermiz Jammo, Sarhad Y. *La Structure de la Messe Chaldéenne du début jusqu'à l'Anaphore: Etude Historique*, 153–4, Orientalia Christiana Analecta, 207, Rome: Pontificium Institutum Orientalium Studiorum, 1979.

[18] Klein, Albertus F.J. *The Acts of Thomas: Introduction, Texts, Commentary*. Leiden: Brill, 1962.

Demonstration 23 #63,[19] sources that predate him. While he devotes several stanzas (stanzas 96–101) to the dismissal theme without giving the whole dismissal formula, he makes clear that the "non-baptized" were put out of the church:

ܠܐܢܫܐ ܕܠܐ ܥܡܝܕ ܦܛܪ ܟܗܢܐ ܗܟܐ ܕܡܬܩܕܫ

"The priest puts out he who is not baptized when the Sanctification takes place (98a)."

ܠܐܢܫܐ ܕܠܐ ܥܡܝܕ ܥܠ ܗܝ ܡܦܩܝܢ ܡܟܐ ܕܡܬܩܕܫ

"On account of this, they put out he who is not baptized once the Sanctification takes place (103a)."

ܘܐܢܫܐ ܕܠܐ ܥܡܝܕ ܠܘ ܒܒܢܝܐ ܦܣܩ ܡܢܬܗ

"he who is not baptized his lot is not among the sons (104a)."

Jacob considers the catechumens strangers to the Father's House, while the baptized ones are part of the household of the Father's House. He takes the former for "deficient" (stanza 97), and worthy of disassociation in the bloodless offering of Christ.

Along with the non-baptized, the hearers (ܫܡܘܥܐ) had to leave the church before the anaphora. The mention of the "hearers" in *mimrō* 95 stanza 117 is casual, but the full formula in which it is found is preserved in the liturgy of the Church of the East: ܙܠܘ ܫܡܘܥܐ ܘܚܙܘ ܬܪܥܐ "Go hearers and watch the doors." According to Narsai's 17th homily, they are the catechumens, and for (Bishop) Sarhad Jammo there is no reason not to believe that they were so, adding that they were responsible of watching the exterior doors of the church.[20] Although Jacob of Edessa leaves the impression that the "hearers" are the catechumens,[21] the earliest Christian sources offer different interpretations. In the

---

[19] Parisot, Jean. *Patrologia syriaca*, vol. II, 133, lines 3–7, Paris: Firmin-Didot, 1894.

[20] Jammo, *La Structure*, 154–5.

[21] Jacob of Edessa's Letter to Thomas the Priest reported by *Dionysius bar Ṣalībī: Exposito Liturgiae*, 6. In fact Jacob of Edessa does not equate the hearers with the catechumens, but he lists those who had to leave the church: 1) the hearers, 2) ܡܬܬܒܠܥܢܐ (energumens), and 3) the penitents. From this context, the hearers must the catechumens.

Didascalia Apostolorum 8, 6 for example, the *akrowmenoi* (hearers) are those who were allowed to attend the readings of the Scriptures without being catechumens,[22] and for Basil the Great and Gregory the Thaumaturge, they are a category of penitents.[23] Since Jacob of Serugh already referred to the catechumens, the hearers in his hymn must be either simple listeners as in the Didascalia or some kind of penitents.

On a more practical note, Jacob is puzzled why some baptized people leave the (long) Eucharistic celebration to return only for partaking the communion, mingling themselves with the "stranger," the non-baptized ones.

Anaphoric Service

Stanza 103 makes a clear reference to the time of the anaphora with the phrase ܡܢ ܕܬܫܡܫܬܐ when catechumens were asked to leave. The phrase is based on the term ܩܘܡܐ, which refers, with ܩܘܪܒܐ, to the anaphora.[24] The first part of this service until Sanctus, including the Creed and the prayer of peace, does not seem to be present in *mimrō* 95. The Introit Prayer, *sedrō da-m'alṭō*, lit. "*sedrō* of entrance [into the sanctuary]," was quite long perhaps due to two processions that used to take place at this time. The first was made by the celebrant and his diaconal entourage, moving from the bema to the sanctuary, and the second, by a deacon bringing the gift offerings from the sacristy and before depositing them on the altar, he had to process them around the church while another deacon incensed before him. While these elements survived in the Armenian Church, in the Syriac Orthodox (and Catholic) Church only the incensing by the deacon (without offering) is performed today.

No mention of the Creed is made and this is also the case with the Prayer of Peace. In his adulthood Jacob must have

---

[22] Funk, F.X. *Didascalia et Constitutiones apostolorum*, vol. I, 478–9, item 2, Paderbornae: In libraria Ferdinandi Schoeningh, 1905.

[23] Hammond, C.E. *Liturgies Eastern and Western: Being the Texts, Original or Translated of the Principal Liturgies of the Church*, 524 (29–34), Oxford: Clarendon Press, 1965.

[24] For the terms see Payne Smith, *Thesaurus Syriacus*, col. 3503, 3725.

witnessed the insertion of the Creed in the Eucharistic liturgy by Peter the Fuller, patriarch of Antioch (died in 488), as documented by the Greek Church Historian Theodore Lector (early 6th century).[25] The Eucharistic Prayer that follows is made of three steps: Eucharistic dialogue between the celebrant and the people, preface, and Sanctus, *qaddīš*, said by Jacob to be "chanted by the crowds" (stanza 122). By the crowds he probably meant the people, as is clear in the commentary of the Eucharist by Bar Ṣalībī: "Now the people shout, saying: Holy, holy, holy, etc."[26] Nowadays, *qaddīš* is chanted by the deacons, sometimes even by one of these.

The anamnesis follows and it is made of three prayers: The Lord's recommendation (*puqōdō d-moryō*), remembrance of the divine economy (*'uhdōn mdabrōnūthō allōhoytō*), and thanksgiving. None of these seems to be referred to in *mimrō* 95.

After the anamnesis is the epiclesis made of 1) the calling of the Holy Spirit to come down on the bread and wine to make them into the Body and Blood of Christ, and 2) "sacramentally" to mix the Body and Blood to become one with Christ. The final prayer by the priest asks for the holiness and healing of the participants by the Holy Mysteries. Jacob of Serugh refers to the Epiclesis, calling it the *rūḥōfō* "hovering" of the Holy Spirit, momentous in the Eucharistic celebration, and dwells on its importance in the context of his exhortation not to leave the service. The wording of stanzas 113–114, 116, and 118 reflects the modern invocation of the Holy Spirit by the deacon to sanctify the bread and wine: "How awesome is this moment and how solemn is this time O my beloved ones, in which the Holy Spirit moves to descend from the high Heaven to hover (*rōḥef*) and settles over this Eucharist that is placed, consecrating it." Shortly after this diaconal prayer, the priest

---

[25] Migne, *Patrologia Graeca*, vol. 86a, 208–10. Seemingly, Jacob of Edessa was not aware of the role of Peter the Fuller, for this is what he says about the insertion of the Creed in the liturgy which took place according to him in the Council of Nicea: "After the Creed of the 318 (Fathers) was written down, it was also judged that it must be added to the rite of the Eucharist (*qurōbō*);" *Dionysius bar Ṣalībī: Exposito Liturgiae*, 7:15–7.

[26] *Dionysius bar Ṣalībī: Exposito Liturgiae*, 53:25–6.

says the following two prayers: "In such a way that, when (the Holy Spirit) descends, he turns this bread into the life-granting body, redeeming body, the body of Christ our God;" "may he fulfill this mixture, *mzōḡō* [Jacob uses the participle *ḥōleṭ*] that is in this chalice the blood of the new covenant, redeeming blood, the blood of Christ our Lord." Interestingly, the epiclesis for Jacob was also the sending of Christ to descend and settle on the bread and wine (stanza 113).

No clear mention is made of the Great Intercessions (ܬܟ̈ܫܦܬܐ or ܕܘܟ̈ܢܐ) although the Catholic Prayer following them perhaps hints at them. This prayer starts with the supplication *anīḥ w-ḥasō wa-šbuq lšūr'ōṭō dīlan w-dīlhūn...* "Give rest, pardon, and forgive our faults and theirs...;" Jacob made clear in stanza 128 that this supplication was said by the entire congregation (nowadays it is diaconal), and this is also confirmed by Bar Ṣalībī.[27] At any rate, the pronominal suffix third masculine plural of *dīlhūn* must refer to the persons mentioned in the Intercessions: The Fathers of the Church, the Believing Brothers, Believing Kings, Spiritual Fathers, Doctors, Ascetics, and the Dead Believers.

Stanzas 131–132 speak of "begging mercy from God" by the congregation. It is not known if these stanzas reflect the prayer "we beg mercy from the Lord" that formerly the deacon used to say after the Great Intercessions and before the Catholic prayer. Bar Ṣalībī who refers to this diaconal prayer says that "(Church) doctors stopped it" because it was superfluous.[28] There is of course the priest's prayer that also begs for mercy: "Let the mercies of the great God and of our redeemer Jesus Christ be with you forever."

The next stage in the modern liturgy is the Fraction (ܩܨܝܐ) and Signation (ܪܫܡܐ), neither of which are specifically mentioned by Jacob of Serugh. At this point, the Royal Gate (nowadays a mere curtain) is closed in order to be reopened at the time of the recitation of the Lord Prayer. Jacob refers to this major prayer several times when he highlights the difference between the baptized ones who are entitled to call God "Our Father", and the

---

[27] *Dionysius bar Ṣalībī: Exposito Liturgiae*, 73:11.
[28] Ibid., 76:8–10.

catechumens who have no right to do so.²⁹ He clearly refers to it in stanza 115, *Our Father...* chanted by the entire congregation as has always been the case up to the present time.

The Lord's Prayer is an invitation to the communion that follows. Jacob mentions the opening of the Gate for communion in the context of some of the faithful who leave the church early in the Eucharistic celebration to return to take communion at this late stage of the celebration (stanzas 138–139, 143). Bar Ṣalībī situated the communion after the Fraction but did not specify after which prayer it began.

In the devotional and sacrificial context after the Fraction, Jacob inserts a prayer that became part of the West Syriac Eucharistic celebration, near its end. The prayer is an exhortation for participants to beg God the Father to accept the bloodless sacrifice of Christ for the forgiveness of sins (162–170). By the time this beautiful exhortation was inserted in the Eucharistic liturgy of the Syriac Orthodox Church, as well as in the Maronite liturgy, a doxology not attested in *mimrō* 95 was added:

> Glory to the Father who delivered his Son for our salvation.
> Adoration to the Son who died on the Cross and gave us life.
> Thanks to the Spirit who began and fulfilled the mystery of our salvation.
> O most sublime Trinity have pity on all of us.

Interestingly, the Church of the East attributed Jacob of Serugh's exhortation, along with the appended doxology attested in the Syriac Orthodox liturgy, to none other than Narsai, the famous 6th century poet and theologian.³⁰ While the whole prayer is not part of the East Syriac liturgy of the Eucharist, it is nonetheless found among several other *turgāmē*-anthems. In fact another prayer

---

²⁹ Bar Ṣalībī is of the same mind: "On account of this, we too as soon as we are baptized, we call Our Father who art in Heaven;" *Dionysius bar Ṣalībī: Exposito Liturgiae*, 83:13–4.

³⁰ *Kṯāḇā d-turgāmē* [The Book of *turgāmē*], 211–2, Baghdad, 1968; repr. Chicago, 1997.

very familiar in the Syriac Orthodox Eucharist Service, ܗܘ ܪܘܚܐ ܐܒܐ ܘܡܢܗ, is also attributed to Narsai.[31]

CONCLUSION

All of the *mimrē* of Jacob of Serugh treat issues relevant to his role as Bishop, and thus they are essentially pastoral in nature. This explains why he was concerned that the faithful, not fully appreciating the Eucharist, forfeited its spiritual benefits by leaving early. He was not alone in his concern and admonition, since the Didascalia chapter XIII [ii. 59] is also an admonition to the faithful to be constant in assembling together. An instruction such as "Make not your worldly affairs of more account than the word of God; but on the Lord's Day leave every thing and run eagerly to your Church…" is echoed throughout *mimrō* 95.

Although *mimrō* 95 is not a commentary on the Eucharistic celebration, and despite the fact that its author did not refer to every stage in the course of this celebration, it nonetheless gives us an idea about how the Eucharistic celebration was conducted at the end of the 5th and early 6th centuries. The few but important stages in this celebration, such as the liturgy of the word and the "hovering" of the Holy Spirit, are part and parcel of today's Syriac Orthodox liturgy, a fact which highlights the ancient character of this liturgy and its originality.

---

[31] *Ktābā d-turgāmē*, 212.

www.ingramcontent.com/pod-product-compliance
Lightning Source LLC
Chambersburg PA
CBHW070522090426
42735CB00012B/2853